LENTWISE

LENTWISE

Spiritual essentials for real life

Paula Gooder

CHURCH HOUSE
PUBLISHING

Church House Publishing
Church House
Great Smith Street
London SW1P 3AZ

Tel: 020 7898 1451
Fax: 020 7898 1449

ISBN 978 0 7151 4165 6

Published 2008 by Church House Publishing

Copyright © Paula Gooder 2008

The opinions expressed in this book are those of the author and do not
necessarily reflect the official policy of the General Synod or The Archbishops'
Council of the Church of England.

Bible quotations from the New Revised Standard Version of the Bible are
copyright © 1989 by the Division of Christian Education of the National Council
of the Churches in the USA. All rights reserved.

Lines (p. 24) from Dietrich Bonhoeffer, *Letters and Papers from Prison,* The
Enlarged Edition 1971, are reproduced by permission of SCM-Canterbury Press

Cover design by Aubrey Design
Inside design by Hugh Hillyard-Parker, Edinburgh
Printed in Wales by Creative Print and Design Ltd, Blaina

Contents

How to use this course

Introduction

What counts as a travel essential? We all have our own pet 'essentials' list for holidays. After a toothbrush and soap what would you put on yours? A book? MP3 player, CD or radio? Camera or video camera? Hair straighteners or a hairdryer? Cuddly toy? Travel essentials range from the mundane (a razor or shampoo) through the luxurious (a cashmere blanket for an aeroplane flight) to the ridiculous. When I surfed the Internet looking for travel essentials I found listed such things as a 'hat retainer' to prevent the wind blowing your hat away; inflatable coat hangers and a waterproof bag for MP3 players for use while swimming. How any of these quite fit in the category of 'essential' is hard to imagine.

If you went on a different kind of journey, however, you would take an altogether different kind of travel essential. Expeditions that involve trekking into the unknown require more 'essential' essentials, like a map or compass, food, a torch, some kind of shelter and water. Real life with its unpredictability and dependence on factors beyond our control has much more in common with an expedition than with a trip to a comfortable cottage or hotel room. Sometimes the sun is shining in our world, the weather is balmy and we have no real worries about our life journey; at other times storm clouds gather, the temperature drops and our destination is foggy. At these times, the spiritual equivalent of essentials for an expedition become vital for our survival. This course will explore five 'spiritual essentials' for real life that will help us to raise various questions that affect all our lives:

● A Compass: Where are we going in life? How do we know where we should be going on life's journey? What life is all about?

● Bread: What nourishes me and keeps me going? What really feeds me?

● Light/a torch or lamp: Where do I get insights about my everyday life? What shines a light in my life and gives me clarity?

● Shelter: Where do I find true security? What makes me feel safe?

● Water: Where do I get refreshment? How do I avoid getting burned out?

There is a story, oft-told by preachers but worth repeating, that goes a bit like this. A minister was speaking at a school and she asked the children: what climbs trees, has a long bushy tail and loves acorns? There was the usual forest of hands as the children were all desperate to give an answer. So the minister chose a pensive-looking boy on the front row, who said 'Well I know the answer must be Jesus because you're a minister but it does sound more like a squirrel to me.' Hardly surprisingly, the answer to the questions outlined in the spiritual essentials list above *is* Jesus but that is only half the answer to the question. Jesus is indeed the answer but what precisely does that mean? How can we learn from Jesus the spiritual essentials for our lives that will mean we can survive life's storms? Could it be that he is the starting point for our questions?

While many passages in the Bible could help us to begin to answer these questions, John's Gospel is perhaps the best place to start. Although the Gospel of John is, at times, the most complex and 'spiritual' of all the Gospels, it also uses down to earth images to describe who Jesus is and what he does. In John, Jesus describes himself using everyday images like bread and light and shows himself to be a perfect example of the spiritual essentials we seek. This course then encourages us all to stock up our store of spiritual essentials so that, in the company of Jesus, our companion on the way, we might face life's storms with courage and hope.

Using this course

Your group

Some of the groups undertaking this course will be well established and know each other well; others may be relatively new or will have come together solely in order to undertake this course. You will probably find that you need to adapt the material in this course to fit the needs of your group. If people know each other well they may feel able to share more personal material than those who do not know each other as well. The material in this course is a resource but does not have to be followed in its entirety. Please feel free to edit the material as best fits your group and its needs. In particular use only the questions/discussion material you need to use and ignore any material that does not fit the context of your group. The course includes far too many discussion questions for any one group. This is to give a variety of questions so that your group can take the material in the direction it finds most helpful.

In addition, the timings given are only guidelines: you can spend as much time as you choose on each section.

Getting ready

At the start of each session is a section that tells you how to get ready.

There is also a reflective piece I have written to get you into some of the issues that arise out of the Bible passage you will be exploring. It would be good for group leaders to have read it before the session and group members are also recommended to read it in advance as it will enable them to tackle the passage and the questions at a deeper level. However, for people who do not have time, the session will work whether or not you have read the reflection.

Following this is a list of things you will need to prepare in advance. Make sure you check the list in enough time to sort them for the group.

It would be good to play some music in the group – at the point indicated in the session – to give people time to reflect on what they have been talking about. You can use any music you choose, though something meditative would be advisable! Either use CDs you have already or, if you would like to buy something, try one of the following:

- *Taizé Chant*, St Thomas' Music Group, Margaret Rizza, 2006
- *Relax*, Classic FM, 2007
- *50 Instrumental Golden Hymns*, Kingsway, 2004 (or volume 2, 2005)
- Rob and Gilly, *Be Still / I Will Seek Your Face*, Diadem Records, 2000
- *New Wine Acoustic Worship*, New Wine (4 volumes available)
- Ruth Fazal, *Songs from the River Vol. 4*, Tributary Music, 2005.

At various points in the session, it is suggested that you play some music. If your group is comfortable with periods of silence, you may like to have silence instead of music; those groups, however, that are less familiar or comfortable with silence may find that music enables them to reflect more easily than sitting in silence would.

Getting started (10 minutes)

Each session will begin with a time of welcome, to help members leave behind what they've been doing and begin to focus upon the topic.

You might like to mark the formal start of the session by lighting the candle that acts as a focal point and to say the opening course prayer.

Then there will be space to reflect on issues that have arisen from the previous session, before a brief topic to talk about in twos and threes to get the group into the theme for that week. Group exercises are indicated by 🌐.

Hearing the word (5 minutes)

Then turn to the Bible passage for the week. Invite someone from the group to read the Bible passage out loud. I have re-translated each Bible passage with the aim of showing fresh insights into the passage. You can, if you find it helpful, invite the person reading the passage to read it from a published translation (like the NRSV or NIV or *Good News*) so that people have the chance to see what is different in this translation. I have often left the translation feeling a little rough. This is deliberate so that you can see a bit more of what the Greek words were trying to get at.

Unpacking the word (5–10 minutes)

After the passage has been read, encourage group members to explore their reactions to it. I have provided a few things you might like to know about the passage (in the section entitled Wordwise), which may help you to unpack the passage a bit.

Remind people that they are not aiming for right answers or for profound insights, but simply for their own reaction to what the passage says. They shouldn't shy away from stating the obvious – often the obvious is crucially important for helping us to get behind what is really going on in a passage.

The following questions might also help you to explore the passage in more detail:

● Is there anything you particularly liked about this passage? Why do you like it?

● Did anything stand out for you from the passage?

● Did anything confuse you?

● How did it make you feel?

Getting down to it (40 minutes)

This is the major part of the session and encourages people to reflect on what the passage might be saying to them in their lives. The questions are designed to help the group explore how the message of the passage might be applied to them. There are normally three questions ⓠ that will help you to open up the subject, though you don't have to stick just to these. Use them as a springboard into the group's overall discussions.

Throughout the session you will find sections containing material for further reflection, marked by ⓖ. These contain a range of quotations and stories relevant to the topic, which are in text boxes alongside the main material, as well as points for further consideration based on the biblical passages. You can bring these in to your discussion if you find them helpful but you can also ignore them if you find you have enough to talk about already.

'Beyond words' (10 minutes)

After the discussion, allow a minute or two of silence and then move into the action. Each week you will be given something to do that will express physically some of the themes you have been talking about. This allows people the space to think differently and the opportunity to come at the questions from another perspective. We recommend that you try to include this, as it will give people the chance to reflect in a different way on what you have been talking about. However, if you find the idea really off-putting (as some of you will), don't worry. You can spend a bit longer in discussion or in intercession (5 minutes on each might be best).

'Into the presence of God' (10 minutes)

Although you have been in the presence of God for the whole of the group session, it is good to end the session reminding ourselves clearly of how God holds us, the whole of our lives and, in fact, the whole world in his hands. This time allows for a time of intercession or of silent prayer in which you offer what you have been talking about – as well as the concerns you brought with you – to God in prayer. In each session there are some suggestions of topics you might like to pray for, alongside any other particular issues that the group may want to pray for.

Closing (5 minutes)

At the end of each session there is a space in the book for people to write down one thing they may wish to take away with them from the session. You may like to invite them to do so and possibly to share it out loud if they feel able to, or to leave them to do it at home.

Round off the session using the responses and prayer provided (or indeed any other prayer that you may prefer to use).

Hints for facilitating your group

Many group leaders using this course will already be experienced in the leading and facilitating of groups. For those of you for whom this is your first time as a group leader or who have done it before but feel a little unsure about what you should be doing, here are some hints and tips for helping your group to go well.

Before people arrive

Check the chairs

It seems an obvious thing to say but, before people arrive, check that there are enough chairs for everyone and that each person will be able to see the other members of the group during the discussion. It is all too easy to focus on content and forget the chairs!

When to have refreshments

Also decide with the host of the group (or yourself if you are the host!) whether you want to begin or end with coffee or tea/biscuits/other refreshments.

- The advantage of beginning with a drink is that people feel relaxed as they arrive; the problem is that it can then be hard to start the group on time. Decide an absolute start time and stick to it!

- The advantage of ending with a drink is that you don't have to worry about running on at the start of the group; the problem is that some people will have to dash away and may miss the opportunity to get to know the other members.

You can of course vary it from week to week (especially if the group is hosted by different people).

Setting a focal point

It can be good to have a focal point in the room (ideally on a table in the middle of the group) for people to look at during quiet moments or to stimulate people to think more visually about the topic you are discussing. If you are going to use the 'action' suggested for each week, you can have that set up on a table in the middle of the room.

Even if you do not do that, try to have a candle (one relatively fat one will last you five weeks) as a way of signalling the beginning and end of the 'formal' part of the group.

You could also think about bringing pictures or objects to put around that fit in with the theme of each week; ideas will be given at the start of each session.

At the start of the first session of the course

Even if you think that everyone knows each other, it is a very good idea to get people to introduce themselves so that no one feels left out. It can also be helpful for those who feel they 'know' people but cannot remember their names to be reminded of names, without the embarrassment of having to ask.

As well as just going round and inviting people to say their names, it is often useful to ask them to say something else. It relaxes people from the start. Ideas of the kind of questions you can ask include:

- What two 'travel essentials' do you always have to take with you on holiday?
- What is the best holiday you have ever had or, if you could go anywhere at all on holiday, where would it be?
- Tell the group something about yourself that they don't already know.
- What is the best book you've read/film you've seen/TV programme you've watched recently?

It can be helpful at the start to invite the whole group to be alert to the group dynamic. People who talk a lot are often unaware of this, so you could say something like:

> Our group will work best if we can all chip in and share our thoughts. Some of you will naturally talk more than others, but try to be alert to others and give people space to speak. If you feel you have been speaking a lot, you may like to choose not to speak for a while to give others a chance.

This can prevent you having to face a particularly talkative person later on in the course (see below under Facilitating a group).

When should the group end?

It is vitally important to agree an end time with the group, especially if you are meeting in the evening. People often will want to get home at the end of the session and need to feel confident that this will be possible every week. The content of the course is designed to last for 1 hour and 30 minutes, but you may want to stay on and talk for a bit at the end. The best idea is to agree a time at which people can leave if they need to, even if the informal chat of the group goes on after this time.

Facilitating a group

As a group leader, you do not need to know everything. In fact, you may be relieved to discover that you do not actually need to know anything! There are no right answers in this course. Your role is to enable people to explore the questions for themselves as clearly and thoughtfully as possible. It can be helpful, however, to come with questions and reflections prepared that will ease your group into discussion.

It is important to value what people say (even if you violently disagree with it). Dismissing what someone says (especially in public) can mean that you destroy or at least undermine that person's self-confidence, and it is important to encourage everyone in the group to value other people's contributions. If you can, find something positive to say about what someone has said – even if it is only 'thank you'! If you want to disagree, try phrasing it as a question: 'Have you thought about . . .?' or 'I wonder how that would affect . . .?' or 'Does everyone agree or are there other ways of seeing this?'

If another member of the group is dismissive of what someone says, it is always good to try to mediate by asking for more views: 'Person 1 thinks this . . . Person 2 thinks that, are there any other ways of seeing it?' If you end up in the middle of a big row, it is probably a good idea to move on and agree to differ on that subject. However, it may be helpful for people if, at the end of the session, you offer to God in prayer the fact that you could not agree. This is a means of honouring the differing positions that exist within the group.

During the group discussion look out for who speaks during the group, how often they speak and how long they speak for.

● Some people will speak a lot.

   This is fine provided that they do not 'hog' the discussion and make it difficult for others to speak or try to divert the discussion into something they want to talk about but is not the focus of the group's discussion.
   If you do have some individuals who talk a lot, then you may need to chip in to the middle of what they are saying and move the conversation on to enable other people to contribute or to turn attention back to the subject in hand.

   If they do not get the hint, you might need to draw them on one side after the group and talk to them tactfully about moderating what they say so that others can also have a chance to join in.

- Some people may speak very little or not at all.

  If you can, it is worth going over the group in your mind after the event to work out whether there is anyone who hasn't spoken. Keep an eye on them and if two sessions go by without their speaking at all, then you may like to direct a question at them during the next session to invite them to speak. If they still seem reluctant, don't press it, as they may not wish to speak out loud.

It is important to recognize that some people are 'reflectors', in other words, they will take it all in and go home and chew over what has been said. This is why it is important to give people the chance to say what they have been thinking about during the week. You may find that the quietest members of the group will return the following week with something profound to say and you need to give them the space to say it.

Another point to be aware of is that, in the course, from time to time I suggest that people turn to their neighbour to talk but always give the option that this can also be done in the whole group. You will need to use your judgement on this:

- Some groups gel quickly and powerfully, and prefer to do all their talking as a large group. However, the danger is that some people are squeezed out of the discussion and never get a chance to talk (or are so shy that they feel unable to speak in front of the whole group).

- Other groups have difficult personalities in them, which means that being asked to talk regularly in twos and threes can be a trial to the ones sitting next to them!

  Keep your eye on what is going on and try to decide what will suit your group best.

The course at a glance

When going on holiday, many of us have certain travel essentials that we feel we must take with us. Many people describe our lives with God as a journey. What then are our travel essentials for our spiritual life? What should we make sure we take with us to help us on the way?

In this course we will explore five different Spiritual Essentials for our journey of faith.

Session 1   Compass: Finding direction
Based on John 14.1-7, this session explores God as our life's destination and Jesus as the Way who helps us to arrive at our destination.

Session 2   Nourishment: Keeping going
Based on John 6.25-35, this session looks at the sustenance Jesus gives us for keeping going in our everyday lives.

Session 3   Light: Gaining wisdom
Based on John 1.4-10 and 5.35-36, this session considers the light Jesus brings into our lives, as well as people, like John the Baptist, who act as lamps for us along the way.

Session 4   Shelter: Finding security
Based on John 10.7-17, this session will help you to discuss the security that Jesus as the gate and the good shepherd offers, and the difference that can make to our lives.

Session 5   Water: Enjoying refreshment
Based on John 4.5-18, this session will examine the living water that comes from Jesus as a source for refreshment in our day-to-day lives.

Note: the Bible passages from John's Gospel are the author's own translation. Other Bible quotations are taken from the New Revised Standard Version (NRSV).

SESSION **1**

Compass: Finding direction

•••••••••••••••••••••••••••••••••

At a glance

Getting started (10 minutes)

Introduction to the course
Opening prayer
Group introduction/opening exercise

Hearing the word (5 minutes)

The passage: John 14.1-7
Wordwise – a few words to think about more

Unpacking the word (5–10 minutes)

Discussion arising out of the passage

Getting down to it (40 minutes)

Group discussion focusing on:
- turmoil and trust
- trusting God
- God our destination and Jesus our life's direction
- direction in everyday life

'Beyond words' and 'Into the presence of God' (20 minutes)

Place a life question on a cross as a symbol of offering it to God
Pray for events around the world

Closing (5 minutes)

Compass: Finding direction

Getting ready

To prepare for the session, you need to read the passage for study (John 14.1-7) and the reflection on the passage below. It is worth providing group members with copies of the course before the first session. We recommend that everyone reads the reflection to help them focus their thoughts on the topic for this session but, if anyone doesn't have the time to do this, they will still be able to take part in the discussion.

More on John 14.1-7

Read John 14.1-7 either in the version set out on page 18 or in your own version before you read this reflection.

Have you ever wished you could have a map of your life? Wouldn't it be useful to know that, next week, your life might get a little bumpy so you need to watch out? Or that there are hairpin bends ahead and, if you do not negotiate them carefully, you could go over the edge? Or, again, that in a few months' time your life will be downhill all the way and you can ease off a bit and enjoy the view? Sadly, however, there are no such 'life maps': we have little or no idea of what is just around the corner until it rears up in front of us.

In this passage in John you can see the disciples grappling with this kind of issue, which for them is made worse by Jesus talking confidently about what is going to happen to him and saying: 'You know the way', until Thomas bursts out with frustration: 'We don't know where you are going so how are we able to know the way?' We might join in with him with our own frustrations: 'Lord, we don't know where *we* are going so how are we able to know the way?'

Jesus' answer to Thomas is also for us: 'Actually you do know where you (and I) are going and you also know the way.' The problem is that we are looking in the wrong places: we want to know what job we are going to have, where we will live, what is going to happen to us, but Jesus shows us something else. We are going, he says, 'to the Father' and THE way there is Jesus. We do, in fact, have a destination in life: God 'the Father' who loves us and yearns for us to be close to him, *and* we have the means of getting there: Jesus, who not only shows us the way but IS the way. We may not have a life-map but we do have a compass: just as on a compass the needle pulls to true north in our lives, Jesus the way pulls to our true north – the Father – and invites us to go along with him.

Jesus' answer is the ultimate big picture answer: the Father is our destination but what about our day-to-day, mini destinations? We all face a barrage of vital questions and everyday small decisions as we make our way through life:

- Shall I go and visit this person or stay at home and watch *Eastenders*?
- Should I accept that job or not?
- Can I justify buying those shoes/that gadget?
- Where should I send my child to school?
- How do I find the right partner for me?
- Where should I live?
- How should I react to that person who has hurt me?

And so on . . .

The answers we give to these questions shape the contours of our lives. How does coming to 'the Father' help us to answer them? The answer must be that our ultimate destination shapes the direction our life takes and all the decisions we make along the way. Our priorities, our hopes and dreams, even our most mundane decisions will be shaped by our closeness to God, who loves us and the whole world so much.

Things you will need for the group

- A candle

- Some music to play

- Music-playing equipment

- If you have easy access to a flip chart, then bring it: there is a group discussion exercise that involves people throwing out ideas that you can write up if you would like to. If a flip chart is difficult, however, you can use an A3 sketch pad or do without and just invite people to say things out loud.

- If you are using a flip chart, make sure you have pens too!

- A wide range of headlines clipped from a recent newspaper covering national and international news

- Two long thin strips of paper that can be made into a cross shape. Mark the vertical strip with N at the top and S at the bottom and the horizontal strip with W on the left and E on the right like this.

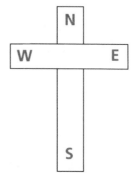

Compass:
Finding direction

Getting started

10 minutes

Introducing the course

As this is the first week, spend five minutes introducing the course. You might like to draw people's attention to:

● the course 'At a glance' page so they can see the overview of the different sessions

● the recommendation that the group members read the 'More on John ...' section for each session in 'Getting ready' to help them think their way in to the each week's session.

Opening prayer

Light a candle, then open the study with the course prayer – either use this one or one of your own

> Loving God,
> be present with us we pray.
> Send your Spirit to open our minds
> to hear your word,
> our hearts to meet you afresh
> and our lives to follow your will.
> W e ask all this through your son,
> our Saviour Jesus Christ.
> Amen.

Group introduction/Opening exercise

As this is the first session, spend five to ten minutes introducing yourselves to each other (see the section headed 'At the start of the first session of the course' in the Introduction, page 7). Even if you know each other well already, you may need to focus your attention on what you are about to do; in this case share with one another what you count as a travel essential, i.e. something you must take with you when you go away, and say why it is so important for you.

Hearing the word

5 minutes

Ask someone in the group to read out the passage: John 14.1-7

You may be helped to know that v. = verse and vv. = verses

vv. 1-3   'Don't let your heart be in turmoil. Trust in God and trust in me. There are many rooms in my Father's house.
If not, would I have said to you that I am going on a journey to prepare a place for you? If I do go on a journey and prepare a place for you, I will come again and take you along with me, so that you are also where I am. And where I am going, you know the way.'

v. 4   Thomas said to him: 'Lord, We don't know where you are going so how are we able to know the way?'

vv. 5-7   Jesus said to him 'I am the way and the truth and the life. No one comes to the Father except through me. If you know me, you will also know my Father and from now on, you do know him and you have seen him.'

Wordwise

- **vv. 1-3** – The word I've translated as **turmoil** here (and other translations give as troubled) literally means 'shaken around'. So Jesus is saying don't let your heart be shaken around by what you think is the uncertainty of what is going to happen.

- **vv 1-3** – The word 'believe' in Greek has within it an element of 'trust', so I decided to use **trust in God and trust in me**. There is a powerful contrast between being 'shaken around' and believing/trusting which has firm foundations.

Unpacking the word

Turn to your neighbour (or if you prefer as a whole group) and choose one of or both the questions below to discuss. If you have discussed in twos or threes, allow enough time to share some of what you discussed with the whole group.

- How did you relate to Thomas' outburst 'We don't know where you are going, how can we know the way?'?

- What do you think it means for Jesus to be 'the way'?

Getting down to it

40 minutes

Turmoil and trust

If you have a flip chart, or something like it, draw a line down the middle of it and put Turmoil on the left and Trust on the right. Invite the group to say the first words that come to mind that describe 'being in turmoil' and 'trusting' (e.g. all at sea; firm foundations).

If you don't have a flip chart, just do one word at a time. Ask people to say out loud words connected to turmoil and then words connected to trust.

Discuss the difference between trust and turmoil. What characterizes trust and what characterizes turmoil?

Thomas was at a point in Jesus' ministry when he clearly felt alone and confused. He knew something was about to happen but had no idea what it was. He was worried about the next step, the direction his (and Jesus') life was going to take. Jesus said to all the disciples, 'Don't have quaking hearts, trust God and trust me' but how realistic a command is that?

> 'I seldom end up where I wanted to go, but almost always end up where I need to be.'
> *Douglas Adams*

Trusting God

Discuss one of or both the following questions:

- How realistic a command is it to trust God and not be in turmoil?

- Do you think Thomas was satisfied with Jesus' answer to him? Does it help you?

I do wonder whether Thomas was satisfied with Jesus' answer to him. Thomas was asking a question about a concrete direction. Where are you going? Where are we going? How will we get there? How will we be able to get there if we don't know where you or we are going?

Jesus' answer was about a spiritual destination ('No one comes to the Father except through me'); he declared the Father to be our destination and Jesus the way by which we get there.

> And when you turn to the right or when you turn to the left, your ears shall hear a word behind you, saying, 'This is the way; walk in it.'
>
> *Isaiah 30.21*

Alice came to the fork in the road. 'Which road do I take?' she asked.

'Where do you want to go?' responded the Cheshire cat.

'I don't know,' Alice answered.

'Then,' said the cat, 'it doesn't matter.'

Lewis Carroll, Alice in Wonderland

Was the cat right?

Like Thomas, many of us want to know where we are going tomorrow or next week but Jesus continues to remind us that he is the way to the Father and this is what shapes the direction of our whole life.

God our destination and Jesus our life's direction

In this passage, the opposite of being in turmoil is believing that we can come to the Father through Jesus.

....

Discuss one or more of the following questions:

- What might our lives look like if we understand our life's purpose as coming to the Father?

- What does it means in practice for Jesus to shape the direction of our whole lives?

- Do you feel that you know where you are going?

....

When I was a child, we went for a walk in the Lake District. Once we got to the top of the mountain, as often happens in the Lake District, the cloud came down and we couldn't see a thing. I remember an overwhelming sense of isolation from the world around – there was just me and my family on the top of a hill in the middle of nowhere – and slight panic. The map with its routes and paths would be no use now – we didn't even know where we were now let alone where we should be going to. Fortunately, however, my mum is a dab hand with a compass and, by the guidance of its shaky needle pointing doggedly to true north, we found our way down the mountain.

> I can't change the direction of the wind, but I can adjust my sails to always reach my destination.
> *Jimmy Dean*

It is this kind of direction that Jesus gives us – we don't need to know where we are now, or even where we are going to, so long as we keep the eyes of our heart fixed on that needle, Jesus, the one who is the way to God, the Father.

Direction in everyday life

Saying that God is our destination and Jesus our direction is quite abstract, but it can have detailed consequences.

Discuss one or more of the following questions:

- What, in life, counts as a small, detailed decision and what as something that indicates our life's overall direction?

- Can your small decisions affect your life's direction? Does your life's direction affect the small decisions you make?

- How much does it matter if we get a few small decisions wrong?

'Beyond words' and
'Into the presence of God'   20 minutes

For this week the action and the intercessions are put together.

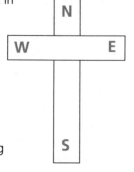

Make a cross out of two strips of paper and place it in the middle of the group as described in 'Things you will need for the group' (page 16).

Give the members of the group a piece of paper each and, while you play some music, invite them to write on the paper a life question that is important to them at the moment.

Then, after five minutes or so, invite them to place their paper on the cross as a symbol of their offering it to the Father through the way of the Son.

Write on a piece of paper a life question or issue that is important for you at the moment (e.g. job, family, home). You can make it as specific or vague as you like.

When you are invited to do so, fold the paper and place your life question on the cross as a symbol of dedicating this question about your life's direction to our destination – God the Father, through the Son.

Keep a moment of silence, and then move into your time of intercession.

Did you know that the word NEWS is an acronym of North, East, West and South and so is more concerned with the fact that stories are gathered from all points of the compass than that it is new?

God's love for the world encompasses each hair on our heads but also the events that affect the whole world. God's care stretches from the smallest issue to the largest event. In your prayers, turn your attention now to world, national and local events.

Take a headline from the selection that your group leader has brought and place it on the cross (you can either place it anywhere on the cross or, if you know where the story comes from, put it at the relevant place – North, East, West or South). Then, either out loud or in silence, bring that place to God in prayer.

Offer the group the headline clippings (which have been cut out of a recent newspaper and represents a world, national or local event in need of prayer) and invite them to place them on the cross and use this as the shape for your intercessions this evening.

Closing

5 minutes

If God is our destination, our lives are being drawn constantly in his direction. If something else is our destination (money, status, promotion, etc.) then our lives are drawn in that direction. The first spiritual essential for real life is having a sense of direction based on relationship with God the Father and Jesus the Son.

Write down on a piece of paper something that you want to take away. It might be a quote, something someone said, something you want to think about some more, an issue about your life's direction that needs more reflection.

Give the group two to three minutes to reflect on what they might want to take away for further thought. As an end to your session, pray the following words together, ending with the prayer from Dietrich Bonhoeffer.

The person leading this part (who doesn't need to be the group leader) should say the words in regular type and the group should say the words in bold:

Don't let your heart be in turmoil

We trust in you our God

Come to the Father, the source of all being

We trust in you our God

Come through the Son, the way, the truth and the life

We trust in you our God

Come in the power of the Spirit

We trust in you our God, we trust in you.

God of the day and of the night:
In me there is darkness,
But with you there is light;
I am lonely, but you do not leave me;
I am feeble in heart, but with you there is help;
I am restless, but with you there is peace.
In me there is bitterness, but with you there is patience;
I do not understand your ways,
But you know the way for me;
Now and for ever.
Amen.

Dietrich Bonhoeffer (1906–45)

At the end of the prayer, if you lit a candle, blow it out to signal the end of the session.

Nourishment: Keeping going

At a glance

Getting started (10 minutes)

Opening prayer
Recap on the last session
Turning to this session

Hearing the word (5 minutes)

The passage: John 6.25-35
Wordwise – a few words to think about more

Unpacking the word (5–10 minutes)

Discussion arising out of the passage

Getting down to it (40 minutes)

Group discussion focusing on spiritual nourishment
Your own spiritual nourishment
Nourishment and priorities

'Beyond words' and 'Into the presence of God' (20 minutes)

Share and eat bread as a symbol of your acceptance of Jesus' nourishment
Pray for each member of the group

Closing (5 minutes)

Nourishment: Keeping going

· ·

Getting ready

To prepare for the session, you need to read the passage for study
(John 6.25-35) and the reflection on the passage, below. We recommend
that everyone reads the reflection to help them focus their thoughts on the
topic for this session, but any who don't have the time to do this will still be
able to take part in the discussion

More on John 6.25-35

*Read John 6.25-35, either in the version set out on page 30 or in your own
version, before you read this reflection.*

What is your favourite thing to eat? Is it something savoury or sweet?
Hot or cold? Fancy or ordinary? Spicy or plain? Nutritious or junk food?
Unfortunately, many of us aren't very good at choosing food that will nourish
us. Many people's favourite foods are laden with fat, sugar and quick release
carbohydrates (you may be an exception but mine certainly are!). In the same
kind of way we are equally bad at choosing spiritual nourishment. We choose
things that will give us a quick boost but have no lasting value; they make us
feel good for a while but quickly fade and lose their worth.

In this passage Jesus points us to what true spiritual nourishment is and
where it comes from. As is often the case in the Gospels, the crowd seems to
misunderstand him entirely and thinks he is talking about physical bread
rather than spiritual nourishment. The people are incredibly keen to get hold
of a loaf of this miraculously lasting bread, since it would make their lives so
much easier.

You can excuse them for their mistake. They have come looking for Jesus
because he has just fed five thousand people miraculously; it is not hard to

see how they might have thought that he was now telling them about a new kind of miracle – long-life bread! But Jesus points out that they have got excited about the wrong thing; they should be much more excited about the prospect of being eternally spiritually nourished by Jesus, who fills us to the brim and answers all our longings (the word for 'be thirsty' in verse 35 can also mean 'yearn for').

One of the intriguing features of this passage is the word John uses for the bread that Jesus gave to the five thousand. John tells us that the bread was barley loaves, the bread of the poor: they were low quality, and hard to eat and digest. In contrast, Jesus is not poor quality, economy barley bread but the bread of life: the best quality available.

His bread is also not like the manna of the wilderness (Exodus 16.1-36). You may remember the story: the people were starving in the desert so God provided miraculous food for them to eat (literally the Hebrew word *manna* means 'what is it?'). The important thing about the manna, however, is that it did not last and by the morning had gone off. In contrast, Jesus, the bread that brings life, lasts not just until the next morning but for ever and ever.

So what kind of nourishment do you look for? Poor quality, economy nourishment, that keeps you alive but little else? Nourishment that's fine while it lasts but is gone in the morning? Or the finest quality, life-bringing nourishment that lasts on and on? When you think back over the kind of spiritual nourishment you have in your life, what is it most like? A dry crust? Junk food that is great while you eat it but leaves you hungry in a few hours? Or something much finer and long lasting that keeps you going through the ups and downs of life?

Things you will need for the group

- A candle

- Music-playing equipment

- Some music to play

- If you have easy access to a flip chart then bring it: there is a group discussion exercise that involves people throwing out ideas that you can write up if you would like to. If a flip chart is difficult, however, you can use an A3 sketch pad or do without and just invite people to say things out loud.

- A large bread roll (even better, some home-made bread if anyone in your group makes it!), on a plate

(NB: check whether anyone in your group has a wheat or gluten intolerance and make sure you have some alternative bread for them.)

SESSION **2**

Nourishment: Keeping going

Getting started

10 minutes

Opening prayer

Light a candle, then open the study with the course prayer – either use this one or one of your own:

> Loving God,
> be present with us we pray.
> Send your Spirit to open our minds to hear your word,
> our hearts to meet you afresh
> and our lives to follow your will.
> We ask all this through your son, our Saviour Jesus Christ.
> Amen.

Recap on the last session

Last week's session reminded us that God the Father is our destination and that Jesus is the way by which we arrive there.

Share any questions, observations or reflections that you have been thinking about this week.

Turning to this session

This week we are thinking about nourishment and what we need to keep ourselves going.

As a group, try to think up your ideal menu for a three-course meal; if you can't agree you might like to have two or three possibilities for each course.

Hearing the word

5 minutes

Ask someone in the group to read out the passage: John 6.25-35.

This passage comes in John immediately after the feeding of the five thousand. We are told that the crowd wanted to make Jesus king by force and so he went away. They caught up with him again in verse 25.

v. 25	They found him across the sea and said to him 'Rabbi, when did you get here?'
vv. 26-27	Jesus answered them and said: 'Amen, amen, I say to you. You are looking for me not because you saw signs but because you ate from the bread and were full. Do not toil away for food that goes off, but for food that lasts into eternal life, which the Son of Man will give to you. For God the Father has marked him with a seal.'
v. 28	They said to him: 'What must we do to toil away over the works of God?'
v. 29	Jesus answered and said to them: 'This is the work of God that you believe the one whom he sent.'
vv. 30-31	They said to him: 'So what sign are you going to do so that we can see it and believe? What are you going to toil away at? Our fathers ate manna in the wilderness, as it is written, "He gave them bread to eat from heaven."'
vv. 32-33	Then Jesus said to them: 'Amen, Amen, I say to you Moses did not give you the bread from heaven but my Father gives you the bread from heaven, the real stuff. For the bread of God is the one coming from heaven and giving life to the world.'
v. 34	So they said to him: 'Lord, always give us this bread.'
v. 35	Jesus said to them: 'I am the bread of life, the one who comes to me will not be hungry and the one who believes in me will never be thirsty.'

Wordwise

- **vv. 26-7, 32-33** – The words **Amen, Amen** are very hard to translate. They literally mean 'I agree' and are normally placed at the end of a prayer as an opportunity for those hearing it to indicate that they agree with what has been said. It is very unusual for someone to introduce a saying with this word and can only mean that Jesus is indicating how strongly he feels about what he is going to say.

- **vv. 26-27; 28** and **30-31** – **Toil away** is not a great translation but I wanted to draw your attention to the fact that this word is picked up over and over again in this passage (Jesus says, 'Don't toil for food that goes off'; the crowd asks, 'How do we toil for God?' and, later, what is Jesus going to toil at so that they might believe? They are all connected (the same word is used) and we need to pick up the connection. The word refers to hard physical labour (the kind you break a sweat over). Notice that the crowd gets distracted by this word and keeps asking about it, more than about the food that lasts for ever.

- **vv. 32-33** – **the real stuff**: literally the Greek says here 'the true bread from heaven' but the adjective 'true' is left to the very end of the sentence, which emphasizes it. I've tried to reflect this here. This is the bread from heaven – the real stuff – as opposed to any other bread that is less 'true', 'genuine' or 'real' than the 'one who comes down from heaven', i.e. Jesus.

Unpacking the word   5–10 minutes

Turn to your neighbour (or if you prefer as a whole group) and choose one of or both the questions below to discuss. If you have discussed in twos or threes, allow enough time to share with the whole group some of what you discussed.

1   In this passage Jesus talks about three different kinds of food:

- food that goes off (vv. 26-27);
- manna from heaven (vv. 30-33) – you might like to recall the main parts of this story from Exodus 16;
- food that lasts into eternal life (vv. 26-27).

How are they similar? How are they different?

2   What do you think food that lasts into eternal life is?

Getting down to it

40 minutes

Spiritual nourishment

Although food that lasts into eternal life is hard to define, it is clear that it is connected to spiritual nourishment. What do you think spiritual nourishment is? Out of your own experience, can you try to identify what characteristics might be particularly identified with spiritual nourishment (e.g. one-to-one relationship; an encounter with Jesus)?

You might like to make a list either on a flip chart or out loud of some of the main characteristics of spiritual nourishment; alternatively you can just discuss it in the group without making a list.

Your own spiritual nourishment

Discuss one or more of the following questions:

- Where in our lives do we find the kind of nourishment that Jesus brings, which is long-lasting and not, to use a modern analogy, like junk food that fills you up to start with and then leaves you feeling hungry?

- In your life, what kinds of thing provide lasting inner sustenance?

- Do you always find sustenance where you expect to find it or are you sometimes surprised?

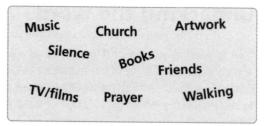

Music   Church   Artwork
Silence   Books   Friends
TV/films   Prayer   Walking

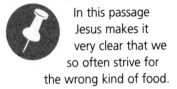 In this passage Jesus makes it very clear that we so often strive for the wrong kind of food.

I would feed you with the finest of the wheat, and with honey from the rock I would satisfy you.

Psalm 81.16

We toil away for nourishment that goes off rather than for food that lasts eternally. It is this long-lasting, deeply nourishing food that keeps us going in our lives of faith.

Far more indispensable than food for the physical body is spiritual nourishment for the soul. One can do without food for a considerable time, but a man of the spirit cannot exist for a single second without spiritual nourishment.

Mohandas Gandhi 1869–1948

There was a great exchange in the *Church Times* a year or two ago. One reader wrote in to the Letters page and expressed the view that sermons were a waste of time since the correspondent had heard many, many sermons but couldn't remember what they were about.

The following week there was a response pointing out that over the space of many years the respondent had eaten many, many dinners. He couldn't remember anything about any of them but he was alive ...

Nourishment and priorities

Discuss one or more of the following questions:

- Do you expect to be nourished in your spiritual lives daily? Weekly? Monthly? Not at all?

- What do you do if you find that you are not being nourished spiritually?

- Do you find yourself constantly running on empty? What might you do to avoid this?

'Beyond words'

With some music playing, hand round a bread roll and invite all members of the group to take a piece and simply hold it in their hand.

While they hold it, invite them to think about the nourishment of their life; after five minutes or so, say the words 'Jesus says, "I am the bread of life"' and invite the group to eat their bread.

When the bread is passed to you, take a piece and hold it in your hand. In silence, give thanks for the way you are spiritually fed and commit yourself to seeking further nourishment in the days, weeks and months ahead.

When the leader says 'Jesus says "I am the bread of life"', eat the bread as a symbol of your acceptance of the nourishment that Jesus brings.

'Into the presence of God'

10 minutes

Part of our spiritual nourishment comes from the support we receive from those around us. Spend some time in silence (or with quiet music playing) praying for the different members of the group.

At the start of their wonderful book *Sleeping with Bread: Holding What Gives you Life* (Paulist Press, 1995) the Linns (Dennis, Sheila Fabricant and Matthew) tell the story of the children who were orphaned and left to starve during the Second World War. Many of those who were rescued and placed in refugee camps were discovered to be unable to sleep at night. Eventually the helpers discovered that, if the children were given a piece of bread to hold, they were able to go to sleep in the guarantee that they would find nourishment in the morning.

One of the things that makes us most anxious is fearing that we will lose the nourishment we need for life.

You may wish to remain in silence for the whole time, or after a few minutes to split into twos and threes and to pray out loud for each other.

Closing

Jesus yearns to give us the highest quality, longest-lasting food for the soul but we so often strive for poor quality nourishment that is past its sell-by date. The second spiritual essential for real life is the eternally lasting bread of life .

Write down on a piece of paper something you want to take away. It might be a quote, something someone said, something you want to think about some more, an issue about your life's direction that needs more reflection.

Give the group two to three minutes to reflect on what they might want to take away for further thought. As an end to your session, pray the following words together, ending with saying or singing the hymn 'Guide me, O thou great redeemer'.

The person leading this part (who doesn't need to be the group leader) should say the words in regular type and the group should say the words in bold:

> In a world of spiritual hunger
> **Jesus says, 'I am the bread of life'**
> To those with no strength to carry on
> **Jesus says, 'I am the bread of life'**
> To those in need of nourishment
> **Jesus says, 'I am the bread of life'**
> To each one of us
> **Jesus says, 'I am the bread of life'.**
>
> *continues on p. 36*

Guide me, O thou great Redeemer
pilgrim through this barren land.
I am weak, but thou art mighty;
hold me with thy powerful hand.
Bread of heaven, bread of heaven,
feed me till I want no more;
feed me till I want no more.
Amen.

William Williams (1717–91) translated by
Peter Williams (1727–96)

(Many of you won't be able to resist singing this – if so,
below are the words to the rest of the hymn!)

At the end of the prayer, if you lit a candle, blow it out to signal
the end of the session.

Open now the crystal fountain,
whence the healing stream doth flow;
let the fire and cloudy pillar
lead me all my journey through.
Strong deliverer, strong deliverer,
be thou still my strength and shield;
be thou still my strength and shield.

When I tread the verge of Jordan,
bid my anxious fears subside;
death of death, and hell's destruction,
land me safe on Canaan's side.
Songs of praises, songs of praises,
I will ever give to thee;
I will ever give to thee.

Light:
Gaining wisdom

At a glance

Getting started (10 minutes)

Opening prayer
Recap on the last session
Turning to this session

Hearing the word (5 minutes)

The passages: John 1.4-10 and 5.35-36
Wordwise – a few words to think about more

Unpacking the word (5–10 minutes)

Discussion arising out of the passage

Getting down to it (40 minutes)

Group discussion focusing on:
● lamps that light the way
● our own call to be lamps
● light in our everyday lives

'Beyond words' and
'Into the presence of God' (20 minutes)

Light a small candle from the larger central candle to give thanks for light
  in your life
Pray for areas and situations that need light and people who give it

Closing (5 minutes)

Light: Gaining wisdom

· ·

Getting ready

To prepare for the session, you need to read the passages for study (John 1.3-10 and 5.35-36) and the reflection on the passage, below. We recommend that everyone reads the reflection to help them focus their thoughts on the topic for this session, but any who don't have the time to do this will still be able to take part in the discussion.

More on John 1.4-10 and 5.35-36

···

Read John 1.4-10 and 5.35-36, either in the version set out on page 42 or in your own version, before you read this reflection.

···

Have you ever woken up in the middle of the night, especially in the countryside where there are no street lights, and tried to walk around without turning on the lights? It can be catastrophic, especially if you don't know the place very well. Night-time forays in the dark mean that we trip over things, stub our toes on unseen objects and even risk falling headlong downstairs (or over a cliff if we are outdoors!). Light, however, is not just important for helping us to see where we are going. It is vital even if we cannot see it. All forms of living creature depend on light for life. It helps plants to grow and provides vital nutrients for our well-being. It is not for nothing that the first sunny day in spring or summer sees droves of us heading outside to bask in the sun's rays.

The two passages from John 1.3-10 and 5.35-36 bring out some of these characteristics of light for our spiritual journey. Jesus tells us that he is the light of the world: not only does he show us the way but he shines on all our darknesses, bringing life and hope where we need it most. In great contrast, John the Baptist is not 'light' but a 'lamp'; he is not the source of light but, kindled from the greater source of light, he does shine in the darkness. John's light does not have the additional power of life-bringing rays but it can show the way.

This contrast between 'light' and 'lamp' can be found elsewhere in the Bible: one of the intriguing features of the creation story in Genesis 1.3 is that God creates light *before* he creates the sun, moon or stars. Here light exists before the sun, which simply acts as a great lamp hanging in the sky, mediating the light that God has already created. In the same kind of way, the new city that John sees in Revelation 21.23 has no need of the sun or the moon because God's glory is its light shining out and illuminating everyone.

We need a lamp, therefore, in our journey through life but we cannot depend just on a lamp for ever. A lamp without the greater source of light might show us the way but it could not renew and enkindle new life in us and the world around us. In fact, if we have the true source of light, we have less or no need of a lamp (you don't need your torch when you are outside in the daytime) since the light itself will lighten our way. We only need a torch when we are in the gloom and away from the light's rays.

This becomes a good analogy for our journey through life. There are times when our lives are in the midst of darkness and gloom. Then we cannot see the way ahead, we stumble over unseen obstacles at our feet and, sometimes, are in danger of falling headlong over unseen cliffs. At these points in our lives, we are in desperate need of a torch or a lamp. Just as John the Baptist provided a lamp for the people of his generation, so we become in need of someone to shine a torch for us in our darkness. However, we must not mistake the torch for the true light. The true light of Jesus alone can shine eternally, bringing life and hope as it shines. All too often we become dependent on the torches brought to us by those we meet and forget to seek out the true source of light.

Things you will need for the group

- A candle (whether you usually light a candle or not for your session, you will need one this week for the 'Beyond words' exercise).

- The same number of tea lights as members of the group and something heatproof to put under them to protect the surface of the table that you will put them on

- Some music to play

- Music-playing equipment

Light: Gaining wisdom

●●●●●●●●●●●●●●●●●●●●●●●●●●●●●●●●●●●●●●●

Getting started   10 minutes

Opening prayer

Light a candle, then open the study with the course prayer – either use this one
or one of your own:

> Loving God,
> be present with us we pray.
> Send your Spirit to open our minds to hear your word,
> our hearts to meet you afresh
> and our lives to follow your will.
> We ask all this through your son, our Saviour Jesus Christ.
> Amen.

Recap on the last session

Last week's session reminded us that Jesus the bread of life gives us true spiritual
nourishment.

Share any questions, observations or reflections that you have been thinking
about this week.

Turning to this session

Many of us will have experienced a power cut at some point in our lives. Either
in the group as a whole or in twos and threes, describe your experience of being
deprived of light and what you found most difficult about it.

Hearing the word

Ask someone (or, here, two people) in the group to read out the passages:
John 1.3-10 and 5.35-36.

John 1.4-10

vv. 4-5	In him was life and the life was people's light. The light shines in the darkness and the darkness cannot overtake it.
vv. 6-7	There was a man who had been sent by God, his name was John. This man came to be a witness so that he might witness about the light so that all people might believe through him.
vv. 8-10	He was not the light but came so that he might witness about the light. The true light, which shines on all people, was the one coming into the world. He was in the world and the world became through him and the world had no knowledge of him.

John 5.35-36

vv. 35-36	That one [John] was a burning and shining lamp and you wanted to rejoice for a while in his light. But I have evidence greater than John's. The works which the Father has given to me to fulfil, these works, which I do, give evidence about me that the Father has sent me.

Wordwise

- **vv. 1.4-10 and 5.35 – light** and **lamp**: the word Jesus uses to describe himself as the light of the world is the generic word for light, in other words the word that is the opposite of darkness; whereas the word that he uses of John the Baptist in verse 35 is an oil lamp that has to be kindled before it sheds light on anything. This makes more sense of John 1.8-10 which claims that John was not, himself, the light.

- **v. 1.5 – overtake**: one of the famous complexities of John 1.5 is how to translate this word. The Greek word John uses here can mean either to take over or gain possession of, or to understand or comprehend. There is an obvious connection between the two: once you have gained possession of something you can understand it better. As is often the case in this Gospel, John clearly means both here. The darkness could neither win against the light nor could it even understand it.

Unpacking the word

5–10 minutes

Turn to your neighbour (or if you prefer as a whole group) and choose one of or both the questions below to discuss. If you have discussed in twos or threes allow enough time to share some of what you discussed with the whole group.

- What does it mean for the darkness to be able neither to take possession of nor to comprehend the light?
- Explore a little what it means for Jesus to be the light of the world. What does it mean about who he is and why he came?

Getting down to it

40 minutes

Lamps that light the way

Who or what have acted as lamps in your life, either showing the way forward or bringing much needed light (or both!).

Share, either in twos or threes or in the group as a whole, your stories of people, events or things (e.g. music, books) that have shed light in your life.

In the C. S. Lewis story *The Silver Chair*, after the children and Puddleglum have released the Prince from the silver chair, the witch returned and tried to enchant them all. The Prince had been kept captive in an underground world that was lit only by lamps hanging from the ceiling. The Queen tried to persuade them that these lamps were the only source of light that existed and that the sun did not and could not exist.

How often do we rely on lamps rather than the source of true light?

Placing John 1.4-10 and 5.35-36 together draws a contrast between the source of all light (Jesus) and lamps or torches who light our way (here John the Baptist).

It is you who light my lamp; the Lord, my God, lights up my darkness.

Psalm 18.28

We cannot hold a torch to light another's path without brightening our own.

Ben Sweetland

The contrast between the two is that Jesus shines eternally, bringing life as well as light, whereas the light that John the Baptist brought was kindled from the greater light and dependent upon it.

Our own call to be lamps

John the Baptist is not the only person called to be a lamp. In Matthew 5.15, Jesus calls each one of us to let our light shine before others.

No one after lighting a lamp puts it under the bushel basket, but on the lampstand, and it gives light to all in the house. In the same way, let your light shine before others, so that they may see your good works and give glory to your Father in heaven.

Matthew 5.15-16

Discuss one of or both the following questions:

● What did Jesus mean by telling us to let our light shine before others?

● What might letting your light shine before others require you to do in your everyday life?

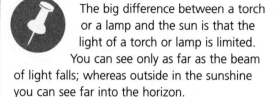

The big difference between a torch or a lamp and the sun is that the light of a torch or lamp is limited. You can see only as far as the beam of light falls; whereas outside in the sunshine you can see far into the horizon.

Better to light a candle than to curse the darkness.
Chinese proverb

And the city has no need of sun or moon to shine on it, for the glory of God is its light, and its lamp is the Lamb.
Revelation 21.23

Jesus says that he is this kind of light that shines further than the eye can see.

Light in our everyday lives

- When the sun shines we rush out to sit in it and bask in its light. How often do you sit in the light of Christ, and what does it entail?

- When you need guidance about something (e.g. about who you are or what to do next) how do you go about getting it? How might the light of Christ help to illuminate the decisions you need to make?

'Beyond words'   10 minutes

If you did not light a candle at the start of the session then light it now.

With some music playing, give each person in the group a tea light (or other small candle), invite them to light it from the main candle and then place the candle around the base of the larger, central candle – don't forget a heatproof mat to protect the surface you place the candle on!

You will be handed a tea light or similar candle. When your turn comes, light your candle from the main, central candle and call to mind someone or something who has been a lamp in your life and give thanks for everything that they have brought to you.

Once everyone has done this, spend a few minutes more quietly looking at the light of the candles and reflecting upon the light that Jesus has brought into the world.

'Into the presence of God' 10 minutes

Continue from here into your time of intercession, focusing this week particularly on:

- areas and situations shaped by darkness, confusion and despair;
- those who dedicate their lives to bringing light to people in their darkness.

Pray for them using either one- or two-sentence prayers or simply the names of places, situations or people for whom you pray.

Closing 5 minutes

Jesus shines as a light in the world enlightening our darkness and showing us who we really are; he also sends other as lamps to lighten our way. The third spiritual essential for real life is light that shines in the darkness.

Write down on a piece of paper something that you want to take away. It might be a quote, something someone said, something you want to think about some more, an issue about your life's direction that needs more reflection.

Give the group two to three minutes to reflect on what they might want to take away for further thought. As an end to your session, pray the following words together, ending either with the Evening Collect from the Church of England's service of Evening Prayer or a Prayer of St Patrick.

The person leading this part (who doesn't need to be the group leader) should say the words in regular type and the group should say the words in bold:

Jesus light of the world

Shine your light on us

In the darkness of this world's night

Shine your light on us

Enkindle the flame of our hearts

Shine your light on us

And send us into the world shining as lights for you

Shine your light on us.

Lighten our darkness,
Lord, we pray,
and in your great mercy
defend us from all perils and dangers of this night,
for the love of your only Son,
our Saviour Jesus Christ.

Amen.

*(Common Worship: Services and Prayers for the
Church of England, Church House Publishing, 2000)*

Or (and especially if you are not meeting in the evening)

The light of God before me.
The light of God behind me.
The light of God above me.
The light of God beside me.
The light of God within me.

Amen.

continues on p. 48

Or, if you prefer, you can say the evening collect in the traditional language form as below:

> Lighten our darkness, we beseech thee O Lord;
>
> and by thy great mercy defend us from all perils and dangers of this night;
>
> for the love of thy only Son, our Saviour Jesus Christ.
>
> **Amen.**
>
> *Book of Common Prayer*

At the end of the prayer, if you lit a candle, blow it out to signal the end of the session.

Important note: Ask each member of the group to bring a symbol of security/sanctuary for next week (e.g. a picture of a place where you feel safe, soft toy, a rock).

Shelter: Finding security

· ·

At a glance

Getting started (10 minutes)

Opening prayer
Recap on the last session
Turning to this session

Hearing the word (5 minutes)

The passage: John 10.7-17
Wordwise – a few words to think about more

Unpacking the word (5–10 minutes)

Discussion arising out of the passage

Getting down to it (40 minutes)

Group discussion focusing on:
- places and situations of safety
- biblical images of security
- safety and risk
- security in life

'Beyond words' and 'Into the presence of God' (20 minutes)

Bring symbols of security to give thanks for safety in our lives
Pray for people in need of safety

Closing (5 minutes)

Shelter: Finding security

Getting ready

To prepare for the session, you need to read the passage for study (John 10.7-17) and the reflection on the passage, below. We recommend that everyone reads the reflection to help them focus their thoughts on the topic for this session, but any who don't have the time to do this will still be able to take part in the discussion.

More on John 10.7-17

Read John 10.7-18, either in the version set out on page 54 or in your own version, before you read this reflection.

One of my favourite feelings is being inside on a rainy, blustery day and knowing that inside my shelter (whatever form is takes) I am safe, dry and warm. This kind of shelter is essential for any form of journey. We need to know that at the end of the day, when we collapse weary from the day's activity, we have somewhere safe in which to rest. This sense of safety is vital for our well-being. If we know that we have a haven into which we can retreat while the rains beat down, the winds howl round about us and the thunder crashes, we can not only survive but face the storms with more courage and determination.

Although we are all much more familiar with the second image in this passage (10.11-17) of Jesus as the good shepherd calling the sheep home, protecting them from wolves and risking everything for their/our welfare, in John 10.7-10 Jesus states that, as well as being a shepherd, he is the gate that provides a safe place for the sheep. This is not all, however. In John 10.7-17 Jesus declares himself to be not only the person who cares for the sheep and brings them home, but a part of that home as well.

The word Jesus uses of himself in verse 7 is a general word for entrance way. It simply refers to the way you can get in to a place. On one level, then, this passage becomes very like John 14.6 that we looked at in Session 1: Jesus is the means by which you can gain entrance. It soon becomes clear, however, that this is not the only meaning here. When we add it to the Good Shepherd saying, it becomes clear that Jesus, as the door, provides safety for those inside. If you have ever watched a film that involves the siege of a great castle then you will know that the most crucial part of the safety of a castle is its doorway. A strong and secure door will keep all those inside safe from their attackers outside. Jesus, the door, welcomes us in but also keeps us safe once we are in.

This is no imprisonment, however. The unfortunate connotation of doors is that they can serve to keep us in against our will, as well as others out and in fact one of the challenges for those seeking to keep others safe is where to draw the line between safety and infringement of liberty (a brief glance at the political complexities involved in counter-terrorism, identity cards and the like can tell you that). Jesus, however, is our place and means of total security, while at the same time also being the way to perfect freedom. He is the door to guard us from danger but also encourages us to come in and out and find nourishment.

Jesus models for us – and indeed offers us – safety balanced with freedom, security with independence, sanctuary with true liberty. We all need in our lives to find this balance that gives us a sense of home without locking us in, a place to rest without undermining our confidence to face the world 'out there'. The shelter that Jesus brings gives us refuge from life's storms but does not expect that we will stay in that haven for ever.

Things you will need for the group

- A candle

- Symbols of security/sanctuary brought by the members of your group

  If you feel that they might forget to bring their own symbol, you might like to have a few spare (soft toys, pictures of sacred spaces, rocks). If you feel creative you could make a visual representation of security/sanctuary in the middle of the room using pictures, rocks, plants or anything else that you can think of; otherwise leave a space (perhaps around the candle?) for people to place their own symbols in the Beyond words section (some groups may even want to make a den!)

- If you have easy access to a flip chart then bring it: there is a group discussion exercise which involves people throwing out ideas that you can write up if you would like to. If a flip chart is difficult, however, you can use an A3 sketch pad or do without and just invite people to say things out loud.

- Some music to play

- Music-playing equipment

Shelter: Finding security

Getting started

10 minutes

Opening prayer

Light a candle, then open the study with the course prayer – either use this one or one of your own:

> Loving God,
> be present with us we pray.
> Send your Spirit to open our minds to hear your word,
> our hearts to meet you afresh
> and our lives to follow your will.
> We ask all this through your son, our Saviour Jesus Christ.
> Amen.

Recap on the last session

Last week's session reminded us that Jesus is the light of the world, who shines in the midst of our darkness and brings us light.

Share any questions, observations or reflections that you have been thinking about this week.

Turning to this session

We live in a world in which safety of any kind is increasingly hard to find. Bearing this in mind, in twos or threes talk about those circumstances or places where you feel safe.

Hearing the word

Ask someone in the group to read out the passage: John 10.7-17.

vv. 7-8	Again, therefore, Jesus said: 'Amen, Amen I say to you, I am the door of the sheep. All those who came before me are thieves and bandits but the sheep did not hear them.
vv. 9-10	I am the door. Anyone who enters through me will be saved and will come in and out and find somewhere to graze. The thief only comes to steal and slaughter and cause destruction; I came so that they might have life and have excessive amounts of it.
vv. 11-13	I am the good shepherd who puts his soul on the line for his sheep. The employee, who is not also the shepherd, does not own the sheep. He observes the wolf coming and neglects the sheep and flees and the wolf attacks them and scatters them, because he is an employee and has no concern for the sheep.
vv. 14-17	I am the good shepherd and I know my own and my own know me, as the Father knows me, I also know the Father. And I put my soul on the line for the sheep. I have other sheep who are not from this courtyard. It is necessary for me to lead these ones and they will hear the sound of my voice and they will become one flock, one shepherd. For this the Father loves me because I lay my soul on the line so that I might take it up again.'

Wordwise

- **vv. 7-10 – door**: the word that is normally translated gate here is simply the general word to describe anything (door, gate, passageway, etc.) through which you pass to get in and out of something. Thus it is reminiscent of 'way' (I am the way, the truth, etc.) as well as reminding us that Jesus provides safety. If you were a sheep with a hungry wolf on its way, a safe door or gate that keeps you in and the wolf out would be just what you wanted.

- **vv. 11-17 – good shepherd**: we are so used to this description of Jesus that it is hard to translate the phrase in any other way. The problem is that the

Greek word means much more than just 'good', which can feel a little like the word 'nice' – bland and undescriptive. The Greek word has a range of meanings that cover beautiful, precious, perfect, noble, morally good, excellent, beneficial, to name but a few. It is therefore an excellent word to describe the way in which Jesus is a shepherd, though it makes it hard to translate.

- **vv. 11-17 – put his/my soul on the line**: As with many of Jesus' images, this phrase is not easy to translate but means something along the lines of 'risking his life'; Jesus puts it down for the sheep and is prepared to die if he needs to.

- Also important is the word that I have translated **soul**. Jesus uses the word life in verse 10 and the word he uses there literally means life; the word Jesus uses in verses 11, 15 and 17 is the one from which we get our English word psyche and refers to our innermost being: Jesus didn't just risk his body for the sheep but everything that he was.

Unpacking the word   5–10 minutes

Turn to your neighbour (or if you prefer as a whole group) and choose one of or both the questions below to discuss. If you have discussed in twos or threes, allow enough time to share with the whole group some of what you discussed.

- Why do you think Jesus uses two images in this passage, that of being a gate as well as being a shepherd? What connects the two images and what is different about them?
- What did it mean for Jesus to 'put his soul on the line' for his sheep?

Getting down to it   40 minutes

Places and situations of safety

If you have a flip chart, or something like it, invite people to suggest words that communicate safety or security to them. Write them up as they say them. These words might be abstract words (e.g. haven, refuge) or places (e.g. church, the beach) or people (family, friends) or things (soft toy, sofa).

If you don't have a flip chart, just ask people to say out loud words connected to 'security'.

When you have done this, reflect together on what connects all these words (e.g. similar emotional state, physical state, relationships, stage of life).

In this passage Jesus provides two different images of safety.

In one he acts as the door that provides a way in for the sheep but also means safety once they have entered; in the other he is the shepherd who nurtures and cares for the sheep, as well as beating off the wild wolves who seek to kill the sheep.

> Safety is something that happens between your ears, not something you hold in your hands.
>
> *Jeff Cooper*

> How precious is your steadfast love, O God! All people may take refuge in the shadow of your wings.
>
> *Psalm 36.7*

Both are images of protection, though slightly different, and serve to enforce the idea that Jesus brings security. Some people have even suggested that the shepherd lies across the entrance to sheep pen, thus acting as a door.

Biblical images of security

Spend some time discussing the range of images of shelter or safety that can be found in the Bible. Which are your favourite ones and why?

> **Psalm 17.8** 'Guard me as the apple of the eye; hide me in the shadow of your wings . . .'
>
> **Psalm 18.30-31** '. . . he is a shield for all who take refuge in him. For who is God except the Lord? And who is a rock besides our God?'

Psalm 18.2 'The Lord is my rock, my fortress, and my deliverer, my God, my rock in whom I take refuge, my shield, and the horn of my salvation, my stronghold.'

Psalm 27.5 'For he will hide me in his shelter in the day of trouble; he will conceal me under the cover of his tent; he will set me high on a rock.'

Matthew 23.37 'How often have I desired to gather your children together as a hen gathers her brood under her wings, and you were not willing!'

Revelation 21.3-4 'See, the home of God is among mortals. He will dwell with them; they will be his peoples, and God himself will be with them; he will wipe every tear from their eyes.'

Plus any others you can think of!

Safety functions on all sorts of levels. In many ways a sheepfold is a good image for the kind of safety that Jesus brings. It provides a sense of home, protection from the dangers around and a place in which to find rest – though the other biblical images of safety that you have just talked about also speak powerfully of the kind of safety we find in God.

In the Old Testament there is an ancient tradition about cities of refuge. If people killed someone else there were laws of limited revenge (an eye for an eye, etc.) that allowed their punishment. So, if they had killed someone, they too would die. If, however, the killing was accidental, then perpetrators could flee to one of six cities of refuge, where they would be safe from revenge, so long as they stayed there. This idea influenced medieval ideas about refuge, which allowed people to claim refuge in churches.

Safety and risk

Discuss one or more of the following questions:

- Is being safe the same as being risk free?

- Is it possible to risk everything while still being 'safe'? If it is possible, what does it tell us about the nature of safety?

- Are there times when it is necessary to risk things in order to achieve safety?

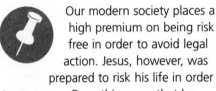 Our modern society places a high premium on being risk free in order to avoid legal action. Jesus, however, was prepared to risk his life in order to save ours. Does this mean that he lacked security or did he find his security elsewhere?

For you have been a refuge to the poor, a refuge to the needy in their distress, a shelter from the rainstorm and a shade from the heat.
Isaiah 25.4

Cowardice asks the question, 'Is it safe?'

Expediency asks the question, 'Is it politic?'

But conscience asks the question, 'Is it right?'

And there comes a time when one must take a position that is neither safe, nor politic, nor popular but because conscience tells one it is right.
Martin Luther King, Jr

Security in life

Discuss one or more of the following questions:

- What kinds of thing do you associate with the word security? Money? Relationships? Career?

- If you looked to Jesus to provide you with security, would this change how you relate to your money, career, etc.?

- What would it mean to look to Jesus for safety? Is it just a nice idea or would it make a practical difference to our lives?

The contrast that Jesus makes between the employee and the owner is as relevant today as it was in the first century.

> Sanctuary, on a personal level, is where we perform the job of taking care of our soul.
> *Christopher Forrest McDowell*

It is only when something belongs to you that you are prepared to risk your life to save it; even the most dedicated employee will find it hard to risk everything for something that belongs to someone else. Jesus' care for us means that he is prepared to go to extreme lengths to ensure that we can find sanctuary – the challenge to each one of us is whether we are prepared to accept the sanctuary he offers or whether we prefer safety of a different kind.

'Beyond words'   10 minutes

In the middle of the group make a space into or on which people can place images or symbols of safety/sanctuary. You can be as creative (or not!) as you choose. It can be an empty space, a space around a candle, something that symbolizes safety or which contains a number of symbols of safety.

Invite people to place the images or symbols of safety that they have brought with them, or to select one from a supply of spares that you brought with you, and to remember and give thanks for all areas of their lives when they have found true safety.

When all have put their image/symbol down, remain quiet for a few minutes, listening to some music.

Hold in your hand the image or symbol of safety/sanctuary that you brought with you. If you do not have one, choose one from the selection the group leader has brought along. You may either place the image or symbol in the centre of the group in silence or, if you feel comfortable to do so, explain to the group why you have brought/selected it.

Either in silence or out loud give thanks to God for all those times in your life when you have experienced true safety.

When all have placed their image or symbol, remain in silence for a few minutes while some music plays.

'Into the presence of God'   10 minutes

Move from here into your time of intercession; remember especially this week all those who are in particular need of safety or sanctuary.

Closing   5 minutes

Jesus provides for us true safety in a world buffeted by danger and anxiety. The fourth spiritual essential for real life is shelter from the storm, brought by the one who is prepared to risk his own life to keep us safe.

Write down on a piece of paper something that you want to take away. It might be a quote, something someone said, something you want to think about some more, an issue about safety that needs more reflection.

Give the group two to three minutes to reflect on what they might want to take away for further thought. As an end to your session, pray the following words together, ending with the prayer from St Augustine.

The person leading this part (who doesn't need to be the group leader) should say the words in regular type and the group should say the words in bold:

O God you are our refuge and our shield
We find our rest in you
You are our stronghold and deliverer
We find our rest in you
You are our rock, in you we trust
We find our rest in you
In you we find shelter from the storm
We find our rest in you.

You inspire us, O Lord, to delight in praising you,
because you made us for yourself;
our hearts are restless until they find their rest in you.
Amen.

St Augustine (AD 354–430)

At the end of the prayer, if you lit a candle, blow it out to signal the end of the session.

Water:
Enjoying refreshment

At a glance

Getting started (10 minutes)

Opening prayer
Recap on the last session
Turning to this session

Hearing the word (5 minutes)

The passage: John 4.5-18
Wordwise – a few words to think about more

Unpacking the word (5–10 minutes)

Discussion arising out of the passage

Getting down to it (40 minutes)

Group discussion focusing on:
● physical and spiritual refreshment
● spirituality and leisure

'Beyond words' and
'Into the presence of God' (20 minutes)

Pour water onto each other's hands as a symbol of refreshment
Give thanks and pray for refreshment

Closing (5 minutes)

Water:
Enjoying refreshment

Getting ready

To prepare for the session, you need to read the passage for study
(John 4.5-18) and the reflection on the passage, below. We recommend
that all the group members read the reflection to help them focus their
thoughts on the topic for this session, but any who don't have the time to
do this will still be able to take part in the discussion.

More on John 4.5-18

*Read John 4.5-18, either in the version set out on page 68 or in your own
version, before you read this reflection.*

Have you ever been on a long walk on a hot summer's day and heard the
babbling of a stream in the distance? There is something about the sound of
bubbling water that suggests coolness, relaxation, but most of all
refreshment. It is hard to resist dangling your feet in the cool water and
feeling the hot sweatiness of the walk melt away (though putting your shoes
on again afterwards is a less pleasant experience!). In some ways food (which
we looked at in Session 2) and water are very similar: both are essential for
life and for keeping us going on the journey. The difference between water
and food, however, is that water can be bathed in as well as drunk and so
gives us refreshment and the energy (both physical and spiritual) to return
once more to our journey.

The well known story of the woman of Samaria is a story of vulnerability and
weariness. The popular understanding of this passage is that this is a sinful
woman in need of Jesus' forgiveness. While this may be the case, the odd
thing is that Jesus makes no mention of her sin or of her need for
forgiveness. Much more obvious is the bone-numbing weariness of both

Jesus and the woman: Jesus has 'toiled' his way to Samaria from Judea in the heat of the sun and is exhausted. The woman, however, has a weariness of a completely different kind: she has had five husbands and now lives with someone else. Whether this was due to something she had done wrong is not revealed in the text (though women in the first century could not divorce their husbands so she may be more wronged than wrong) but what does seem clear is that, in the face of the one, Jesus, who is pure truth she discovered she had nothing left to hide.

She was shaken into honesty by her conversation with Jesus – something for which Jesus commends her ('You spoke well' and 'What you have said is the truth', vv. 17-18). The image I have of this unnamed woman is of someone so numb and bruised by life that she has no energy left to conceal anything from this stranger who appears by the well. Jesus may have been in need of refreshment but it turns out that the Samaritan woman is even more in need of it than Jesus is: Jesus' exhaustion is temporary and physical, whereas the woman's exhaustion is lifelong and both emotional and spiritual.

It is into this context that Jesus speaks a promise of deep, eternally lasting refreshment. There is a play on words going on in the text (which is something the Gospel of John loves to do) that focuses on springs, wells and living water. At the start of the story we are told that Jacob's well is a spring beside which Jesus rests (which it certainly was) but later on in Jesus' conversation with the woman it is called a 'well'. The difference between the two is that a spring is the source of water that bubbles naturally from the ground; a well is a human construction built around water to make it easy to draw it. Although Jacob's Well was originally a spring, it is now a well, constructed by humans and so less 'living' than at first.

In contrast, Jesus offers a spring with living water (i.e. constantly moving water rather than stagnant) but this spring is internal, rather than external and brings eternal rather than simply physical life. Most important of all, it provides eternal refreshment that you can carry within you so you do not have to toil carrying a heavy water jar all the time. Jesus offers us constant, eternal, living and life-giving refreshment. As with all the other spiritual essentials explored in this course, the challenge each one of us faces is to ask ourselves whether we have accepted and packed this essential for the journey or whether, because of distraction, busy-ness or a range of other reasons, we have left this essential behind us somewhere along the way.

Things you will need for the group

- A candle
- A large bowl of water
- A towel
- Some music to play
- Music-playing equipment
- You may also like to bring a symbol (a picture or actual thing) of the other spiritual essentials we have looked at in this course (compass, bread, light, shelter) for the final prayers/reflections today

SESSION 5

Water: Enjoying refreshment

Getting started

10 minutes

Opening prayer

Light a candle, then open the study with the course prayer – either use this one or one of your own:

> Loving God,
> be present with us we pray.
> Send your Spirit to open our minds to hear your word,
> our hearts to meet you afresh
> and our lives to follow your will.
> We ask all this through your son, our Saviour Jesus Christ.
> Amen.

Recap on the last session

Last week's session reminded us of the shelter and sanctuary that Jesus brings.

Share any questions, observations or reflections that you have been thinking about this week.

Thinking about this week

When you are hot and sweaty on a sweltering summer's day, what do you do (or failing that, what do you want to do) to make yourself feel better?

Hearing the word

Ask someone in the group to read out the passage: John 4.5-18.

v. 5	Therefore, he came to the city of Samaria – the one called Sychar – near the place that Jacob gave to his son Joseph.
v. 6	The spring of Jacob was there. Therefore Jesus, who had toiled away on the journey, was sitting by the spring. It was about the sixth hour.
vv. 7-8	A woman from Samaria came to draw water. Jesus said to her 'Give me a drink.' (For his disciples had gone away into the city to buy food.)
v. 9	Therefore the Samaritan woman said to him 'How do you – a Jew – ask me – a Samaritan woman – for a drink?' (For Jews don't have anything to do with Samaritans.)
v. 10	Jesus answered and said to her: 'If you understood the gift of God and who is the one saying to you "give me a drink" you would ask him and he would give to you living water.'
vv. 11-12	The woman said to him: 'Lord, you don't have a bucket and the well is deep so where have you got living water from? You're not greater than our Father Jacob . . . are you? He gave us this well and drank from it – he, his sons and his animals.'
vv. 13-14	Jesus answered and said to her: 'Everyone who drinks from this water will be thirsty again but whoever drinks from the water that I will give will not be thirsty into eternity. The water which I will give will become in them a spring of water bubbling up into eternal life.'
v. 15	The woman said to him: 'Lord, give me this water so that I might not be thirsty nor come through here to draw [water].'
v. 16	Jesus said: 'Go, summon your husband and come back here.'
v. 17	The woman answered and said to him: 'I don't have a husband.'
	Jesus said to her: 'You spoke well that "I do not have a husband".'
v. 18	For you have had five husbands and the one whom you have now is not your husband. What you said is the truth.

Wordwise

- **vv. 6, 11-12 and 13-14 – spring** and **well**: John uses two different words in this passage. In v. 6, when Jesus first arrives at the place, it is called a spring, but thereafter when Jesus and the woman speak to each other, they call it a well. The word spring is used again only in verses 13-14, when Jesus talks about people having a living spring in them. Why do you think he moves from spring to well and back again?

- **v. 6 – toiled away**: the word that I have translated 'toiled away' and which is often translated as 'tired' or 'wearied' literally means to engage in hard physical labour so that one is worn out. In this passage – unusually in John, where Jesus is more often portrayed as the divine Word of God than as a suffering human – Jesus is affected by sheer physical exhaustion and has to sit down.

- **v. 6 – the sixth hour**: no one is quite sure how to count the time systems that the Gospel writer uses but, if the day began about 6 a.m., then the sixth hour would be about 12 noon, the hottest time of the day.

- **v. 15 – water** isn't actually in the Greek but it makes sense of the passage to put it in.

Unpacking the word   5–10 minutes

Turn to your neighbour (or if you prefer as a whole group) and choose one of or both the questions below to discuss. If you have discussed in twos or threes, allow enough time to share with the whole group some of what you discussed.

- Why is water such a good image to describe what Jesus is talking about here?
- What do you think Jesus means both by living water and by water that bubbles up into eternal life?

Getting down to it   40 minutes

Note: *There is marginally less time for discussion this week as the closing activity, which reviews the whole course, will take slightly longer.*

Physical and spiritual refreshment

Water refreshes us both by quenching our thirst and by washing away the grime of day-to-day living.

Discuss one or more of the following questions:

- Remember a time (and then tell the group) when you have felt deeply and truly refreshed. Compare the group's experiences and see what they have in common.
- Is there a connection between physical and spiritual refreshment?
- Do you notice any difference in the quality of your decisions and/or relationships before and after the times of refreshment you talked about above?

Part of what makes a bubbling stream or fountain playing in the breeze so attractive is the fact that it is leisurely.

There is more refreshment and stimulation in a nap, even of the briefest, than in all the alcohol ever distilled.

Ovid

To sit in the shade on a fine day and look upon verdure is the most perfect refreshment.

Jane Austen, Mansfield Park

Now as they went on their way, he entered a certain village, where a woman named Martha welcomed him into her home. She had a sister named Mary, who sat at the Lord's feet and listened to what he was saying. But Martha was distracted by her many tasks; so she came to him and asked, 'Lord, do you not care that my sister has left me to do all the work by myself? Tell her then to help me.' But the Lord answered her, 'Martha, Martha, you are worried and distracted by many things; there is need of only one thing. Mary has chosen the better part, which will not be taken away from her.'

Luke 10.38-42

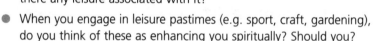

There is a strong connection between leisure, play and refreshment. This is something that Jesus was aware of in his ministry: he regularly went away by himself to pray and he commended Mary for sitting and listening to him rather than being distracted by tasks. Leisure is as important to our spiritual lives as action. We need both: just action leads to burn-out and just leisure to lethargy.

Spirituality and leisure

- If you were to play or be at leisure more in your spiritual life, what kinds of thing might you do?
- When you think about your spiritual life, is it 'hard work' or is there any leisure associated with it?
- When you engage in leisure pastimes (e.g. sport, craft, gardening), do you think of these as enhancing you spiritually? Should you?

The whole discussion between Jesus and the Samaritan woman is based on a play on words. A spring is made up of water that is constantly moving and bubbling and is the opposite of a pond, which contains stagnant or dead water. In this passage Jesus explores the idea of 'living water' as water that not only moves but which also gives eternal life to others.

> When you put your hand in a flowing stream you touch the last that has gone before and the first of what is still to come.
>
> *Anon*

> Do not be wise in your own eyes; fear the Lord, and turn away from evil. It will be a healing for your flesh and a refreshment for your body.
>
> *Proverbs 3.7-8*

One of the most important features of this story is that the Samaritan woman's encounter with Jesus caused her to tell all her neighbours what had happened to her so that they also believed in him, and so she becomes an example of the way in which proper refreshment refreshes the recipient but then goes on to flow outwards to all those around.

'Beyond words'

10 minutes

In the middle of the group place a large bowl of water and a towel. Say the words 'May streams of living water flow within you' and then invite each member of the group in turn to dip their fingers, or whole hand, in the water.

The group leader will say the words 'May streams of living water flow within you' and then will invite each of you in turn to dip your fingers or whole hand in the water. Do this slowly and thoughtfully and, as you do it, reflect on your need for refreshment both spiritually and physically.

When all have dipped their hand in the water, remain in silence for a few minutes while some music plays.

'Into the presence of God'

10 minutes

Move from here into your time of intercession, use the intercessions to:

- give thanks to God for those times in your life (whether regular or rare) when you have experienced true refreshment;
- pray that the refreshment you do enjoy might flow outwards to those around you;
- remember those known to you in need of refreshment.

Closing

5 minutes

Jesus gives us the living water that quenches our thirst, brings refreshment and flows from us to all those around. The fifth and final spiritual essential for real life is living water.

The session ends slightly differently this week.

Say the response below. As usual, the person leading this part (who doesn't need to be the group leader) should say the words in regular type and the group should say the words in bold.

As you say the responses, you might like to make sure that a symbol of each of the spiritual essentials is in the middle of the group.

As we go on our way, we take with us . . .

A compass for direction

You are the way, the truth and the life

Bread to nourish us

You are the bread of life

Light to lighten our path

You are the light of the world

Shelter to keep us from harm

You are the gate and the good shepherd

Water to refresh us

You give us living water. Amen.

Spend a few minutes reflecting on the five essentials we have explored. Which ones do you feel you have already with you on the way? Which ones do you need more of? Which ones are you most in need of now in your life? Write down on a piece of paper those that you feel the need to concentrate on for the next stage of the journey.

Give the group two to three minutes to reflect on what they might want to take away from the whole course. As a group spend a few minutes reflecting upon which spiritual essentials you have found most powerful and what, if anything, you might do differently in your life from now on.

Bring your time together to a close with the words of the Lord's Prayer.

We say together the words that Jesus taught us:

Our Father, which art in heaven,

hallowed be thy name;

thy kingdom come;

thy will be done,

in earth as it is in heaven.

Give us this day our daily bread.

And forgive us our trespasses,

as we forgive them that trespass against us.

And lead us not into temptation;

but deliver us from evil.

[For thine is the kingdom,

the power, and the glory,

For ever and ever.

Amen.]

At the end of the prayer, if you lit a candle, blow it out to signal the end of the group.